ALTAR AND PEW

THE POCKET POETS

THE POCKET POETS

★

JOHN BETJEMAN
A Selection

NEW VOICES
Selected by Alan Pryce-Jones

RICHARD CHURCH
A Selection

LEWIS CARROLL
Comic Verse

COUNTRY POEMS
Selected by Geoffrey Grigson

ROCHESTER
Selected by Ronald Duncan

CHRISTINA ROSSETTI
Selected by Naomi Lewis

TENNYSON
Selected by Raymond Mortimer

D. H. LAWRENCE
Love Poems

ELIZABETHAN LOVE LYRICS
Selected by John Hadfield

GEORGIAN POETS
Selected by Alan Pryce-Jones

THE POCKET POETS

ALTAR AND PEW
CHURCH OF ENGLAND
VERSES

EDITED BY
JOHN BETJEMAN

LONDON: EDWARD HULTON

FIRST PUBLISHED IN 1959 BY
E. HULTON AND COMPANY LIMITED
HULTON HOUSE · FLEET STREET
LONDON E.C.4
MADE AND PRINTED IN GREAT BRITAIN BY
PURNELL AND SONS, LTD.
PAULTON (SOMERSET) AND LONDON

INTRODUCTION

This anthology is confined to descriptions of churches, their priests and people. It is not intended as a book of devotional poems. I had hoped to find some English pre-Reformation poetry describing the look of a church, but descriptive poetry, particularly of buildings, is a fairly late phenomenon. Even in the seventeenth century it appears as only incidental to the main theme of a poem. In Herbert and Traherne it is possible to imagine the Laudian interiors hinted at in the poems and even to find the buildings themselves among those few remote parish churches and private chapels of almshouses, colleges and country houses which have escaped "restoration".

In the middle of the eighteenth century, when poets stepped back to look at the antique fanes whose towers and spires romantically o'ertopped the billowing elms, we have the beginnings of descriptions of these places as buildings. The churchyard usually first attracted attention. So many descriptive poets of that century and the next were country parsons that it is not surprising to find poems about the characters of curates, incumbents and rites as well as about the buildings.

The Tractarian movement provided more devotional poetry than descriptive. The age of unbelief, which started in the nineteenth century and now seems to be on the wane, provided many a wistful lyric of which Thomas Hardy's 'Afternoon Service at Mellstock' is a fine sample. By contrast I was tempted to include one of those exotic poems by Edmund John hinting at some incense-laden high church in an Edwardian suburb, but decided that the theme of one of the best ones, 'The Acolyte', might have been too unhealthy and remote for modern understanding.

There is very little descriptive poetry of Nonconformist

places of worship outside Browning's magnificent 'Easter Day' nor of Roman Catholic churches, so I decided to keep the selection Anglican and to let the Anglo-Catholic movement of the present century be represented by what it is good at in the descriptive vein—light satiric verse. The last poem in the book, Philip Larkin's 'Church Going', moves from the wistful fatalism of Hardy to the more positive longing for faith.

JOHN BETJEMAN

Acknowledgement is made to Mr. Edmund Blunden for permission to include his poem 'Bells', to Macmillan & Company and the Trustees of the Hardy Estate for permission to include the poem by Thomas Hardy, to the Marvell Press for permission to include Mr. Philip Larkin's 'Church Going', and to the executors of John Meade Falkner for permission to include 'After Trinity'.

THE ALTAR

A BROKEN Altar, Lord, thy servant reares,
Made of a heart, and cimented with teares:
  Whose parts are, as thy hand did frame;
  No workmans toole hath touch'd the same.
          A heart alone
          Is such a stone,
          As nothing but
          Thy power doth cut.
          Wherefore each part
          Of my hard heart
          Meets in this frame,
          To praise thy Name:
  That, if I chance to hold my peace,
These stones to praise thee may not cease.
  O lett thy blessed sacrifice be mine,
  And sanctify this Altar to be thine.

THE REVD. GEORGE HERBERT, *The Temple,* 1633

THE CHURCH-FLOORE

Mark you the floore? that square and speckel'd stone,
    Which looks so firme and strong,
        Is *Patience*:

And th'other black and grave, wherewith each one
    Is checker'd all along,
        Humility:

The gentle rising, which on either hand
    Leads to the Quire above,
        Is *Confidence*:

But the sweet cement, which in one sure band
    Ties the whole frame, is *Love*
        And *Charity*.

Hither sometimes *Sinne* steals, and staines
The Marbles neat, and curious veins:
But all is cleansed, when the Marble weeps.
Sometimes Death, puffing at the doore,
Blows all the dust about the floore:
But while he thinkes to spoile the roome, he sweeps.
Blest be the *Architect*, whose art
Could build so strong in a weake heart.

THE REVD. GEORGE HERBERT, *The Temple*, 1633

THE WINDOWES

Lord, how can Man preach thy eternal word?
    He is a brittle crazy glasse:
Yet in thy *Temple* thou dost him afford
      This glorious and transcendent place,
      To be a window through thy grace.

But when thou dost anneale in glasse thy story,
    Making thy life to shine within
The holy Preachers; then the light and glory
      More reverend grows, & more doth win:
      Which els shows watrish, bleake, & thin.

Doctrine and life, colours and light, in one
    When they combine and mingle, bring
A strong regard and awe: but speech alone
      Doth vanish like a flaming thing,
      And in the eare, not conscience ring.

THE REVD. GEORGE HERBERT, *The Temple,* 1633

BEAUTY IN WORSHIP

From A Poem, in defence of the decent Ornaments of Christ-Church, Oxon, occasioned by a Banbury brother, who called them Idolatries.

You that prophane our windows with a tongue
Set like some clock on purpose to go wrong;
Who when you were at Service sigh'd, because
You heard the Organs musick not the Dawes:
Pittying our solemn state, shaking the head
To see no ruines from the floor to the lead:
To whose pure nose our Cedar gave offence,
Crying it smelt of Papists frankincense:
Who, walking on our Marbles, scoffing said
"Whose bodies are under these Tombstones laid?"
Counting our Tapers works of darknesse; and
Choosing to see Priests in blue-aprons stand
Rather than in rich Copes which shew the art
Of *Sisera's* prey Imbrodred in each part:
Then when you saw the Altars Bason said
"Why's not the Ewer on the Cupboards head?"
Thinking our very Bibles too prophane,
Cause you ne'er bought such Covers in *Ducklane*.
Loathing all decency, as if you'd have
Altars as foule and homely as a Grave.
Had you one spark of reason, you would finde
Your selves like Idols to have eyes yet blind.
'Tis onely some base niggard Heresie
To think Religion loves deformity.
Glory did never yet make God the lesse,
Neither can beauty defile holinesse.
Whats more magnificent than Heaven? yet where
Is there more love and piety than there?

My heart doth wish (wer't possible) to see
Pauls built with pretious stones and porphery:
To have our Halls and Galleries outshine
Altars in beauty, is to deck our swine
With Orient Pearl, whilst the deserving Quire
Of God and Angels wallow in the mire:
Our decent Copes onely distinction keep
That you may know the Shepheard from the sheep,
As gaudy letters in the Rubrick shew
How you may holi-dayes from lay-dayes know:
Remember *Aarons* Robes and you will say
Ladies at Masques are not so rich as they.
Then are th' Priests words like thunderclaps when he
Is lightning like rayed round with Majesty.
May every Temple shine like those of *Nile*,
And still be free from Rat or Crocodile.
But you will urge both Priest and Church should be
The solemne patterns of humility.
Do not some boast of rags? Cynicks deride
The pomp of Kings but with a greater pride.
Meeknesse consists not in the cloaths but heart,
Nature may be vainglorious well as art;
We may as lowly before God appear
Drest with a glorious pearl as with a tear;
In his high presence where the Stars and Sun
Do but Eclipse there's no ambition.
Colours are here mix'd so, that Rainbows be
(Compared) but clouds without variety.
Art here is Natures envy: this is he,
Not *Paracelsus*, that by Chymistry
Can make a man from ashes, if not dust,
Producing off-springs of his mind not lust.

ANONYMOUS, *Parnassus Biceps*, 1656

[11]

ON CHRISTMAS DAY

Shall Dumpish Melancholy spoil my Joys
      While Angels sing
      And Mortals ring
   My Lord and Savior's Praise!
Awake from Sloth, for that alone destroys,
'Tis Sin defiles, 'tis Sloth puts out thy Joys.
  See how they run from place to place,
  And seek for Ornaments of Grace;
  Their Houses deckt with sprightly Green,
  In Winter makes a Summer seen;
      They Bays and Holly bring
      As if 'twere Spring!

Shake off thy Sloth, my drouzy Soul, awake;
      With Angels sing
      Unto thy King,
   And pleasant Musick make;
Thy Lute, thy Harp, or else thy Heart-strings take,
And with thy Musick let thy Sense awake.
  See how each one the other calls
  To fix his Ivy on the walls,
  Transplanted there it seems to grow
  As if it rooted were below:
      Thus He, who is thy King,
      Makes Winter, Spring.

Shall Houses clad in Summer-Liveries
      His Praises sing
      And laud thy King,
   And wilt not thou arise?

Forsake thy Bed, and grow (my Soul) more wise,
Attire thy self in cheerful Liveries:
   Let pleasant Branches still be seen
   Adorning thee, both quick and green;
   And, which with Glory better suits,
   Be laden all the Year with Fruits;
       Inserted into Him,
         For ever spring.

'Tis He that Life and Spirit doth infuse:
       Let ev'ry thing
       The Praises sing
   Of *Christ* the King of Jews;
Who makes things green, and with a Spring infuse
A Season which to see it doth not use:
   Old Winter's Frost and hoary hair,
   With Garland's crowned, Bays doth wear;
   The nipping Frost of Wrath b'ing gone,
   To Him the Manger made a Throne,
      Due Praises let us sing,
        Winter and Spring.

See how, their Bodies clad with finer Cloaths,
       They now begin
       His Praise to sing
   Who purchas'd their Repose:
Wherby their inward Joy they do disclose;
Their Dress alludes to better Works than those:
   His gayer Weeds and finer Band,
   New Suit and Hat, into his hand
   The Plow-man takes; his neatest Shoes,
   And warmer Gloves, he means to use:
      And shall not I, my King,
        Thy Praises sing?

See how their Breath doth smoke, and how they haste
          His Praise to sing
          With Cherubim;
          They scarce a Break-fast taste;
But through the Streets, lest precious Time should waste,
When Service doth begin, to Church they haste.
   And shall not I, Lord, come to Thee,
   The Beauty of thy Temple see?
   Thy Name with Joy I will confess,
   Clad in my Saviour's Righteousness;
      'Mong all thy Servants sing
        To Thee my king.

'Twas thou that gav'st us Cause for fine Attires;
          Ev'n thou, O King,
          As in the Spring,
       Dost warm us with thy fires
Of Love: Thy Blood hath bought us new Desires;
Thy Righteousness doth cloath with new Attires.
   Both fresh and fine let me appear
   This Day divine, to close the Year;
   Among the rest let me be seen
   A living Branch and always green,
      Think it a pleasant thing
        Thy Praise to sing.

At break of Day, O how the Bells did ring!
          To thee, my King,
          The Bells did ring;
       To thee the Angels sing:
Thy Goodness did produce this other Spring,
For this it is they make the Bells to ring:

The sounding Bells do through the Air
Proclaim thy Welcome far and near;
While I alone with Thee inherit
All these Joys, beyond my Merit.
   Who would not always sing
    To such a King?

I all these Joys, above my Merit, see
    By Thee, my King,
    To whom I sing,
   Entire convey'd to me.
My Treasure, Lord, thou mak'st the People be
That I with pleasure might thy Servants see.
  Ev'n in their rude external ways
  They do set forth my Savior's Praise,
  And minister a Light to me;
  While I by them do hear to Thee
    Praises, my Lord and King,
     Whole Churches ring.

Hark how remoter Parishes do sound!
    Far off they ring
    For thee, my King,
   Ev'n round about the Town:
The Churches scatter'd over all the Ground
Serve for thy Praise, who art with Glory crown'd.
  The City is an Engine great
  That makes my Pleasure more compleat;
  The Sword, the Mace, the Magistrate,
  To honor Thee attend in State;
    The whole Assembly sings;
    The Minster rings.

THOMAS TRAHERNE, *Poems of Felicity, c.* 1670

[15]

THE DOMESTIC CHAPLAIN

SOME think themselves exalted to the Sky,
If they light in some noble Family:
Diet, an Horse, and thirty pounds a year,
Besides th'advantage of his Lordships ear,
The credit of the business, and the State,
Are things that in a Youngster's Sense sound great.
Little the unexperienc'd Wretch does know,
What slavery he oft must undergo:
Who tho in silken Scarf, and Cassock drest,
Wears but a gayer Livery at best:
When Dinner calls, the Implement must wait
With holy Words to consecrate the Meat:
But hold it for a Favour seldom known,
If he be deign'd the Honor to sit down.
Soon as the Tarts appear, *Sir Crape*, withdraw!
Those Dainties are not for a spiritual Maw:
Observe your distance, and be sure to stand
Hard by the Cistern with your Cap in hand:
There for diversion you may pick your Teeth,
Till the kind Voider comes for your Relief:
For meer Board-wages such their Freedom sell,
Slaves to an Hour, and Vassals to a Bell:
And if th'enjoyment of one day be stole,
They are but Pris'ners out upon Parole:
Always the marks of slavery remain,
And they, tho loose, still drag about their Chain . . .

JOHN OLDHAM, *A Satyr address'd to a Friend that is
about to leave the University, and come abroad in the World,*
in *Works*, 1686

[16]

BLOUZELINDA'S FUNERAL

To show their love, the neighbours far and near,
Follow'd with wistful look the damsel's bier.
Sprigg'd rosemary the lads and lasses bore,
While dismally the Parson walk'd before.
Upon her grave the rosemary they threw,
The daisie, butter-flow'r and endive blue.

After the good man warn'd us from his text,
That none cou'd tell whose turn would be the next;
He said, that heav'n would take her soul, no doubt,
And spoke the hour-glass in her praise—quite out.

To her sweet mem'ry flow'ry garlands strung,
O'er her now empty seat aloft were hung.
With wicker rods we fenc'd her tomb around,
To ward from man and beast the hallow'd ground,
Lest her new grave the Parson's cattle raze,
For both his horse and cow the church-yard graze.

Now we trudg'd homeward to her mother's farm,
To drink new cyder mull'd, with ginger warm.
For gaffer *Tread-well* told us by the by,
Excessive sorrow is exceeding dry.

JOHN GAY, *The Shepherd's Week*, 1714

THE CHURCH-YARD AT NIGHT

SEE yonder Hallow'd Fane! the pious Work
Of Names once fam'd, now dubious or forgot,
And buried 'midst the Wreck of Things which were:
There lie interr'd the more illustrious Dead.
The Wind is up: Hark! how it howls! Methinks
Till now, I never heard a Sound so dreary:
Doors creak, and Windows clap, and Night's foul Bird
Rook'd in the Spire screams loud: The gloomy Isles
Black-plaster'd, and hung round with Shreds of 'Scutcheons
And tatter'd Coats of Arms, send back the Sound
Laden with heavier Airs, from the low Vaults
The Mansions of the Dead. Rous'd from their Slumbers
In grim Array the grizly Spectres rise,
Grin horrible, and obstinately sullen
Pass and repass, hush'd as the Foot of Night.
Again! the Screech-Owl shrieks: Ungracious Sound!
I'll hear no more, it makes one's Blood run chill.

Quite round the Pile, a Row of Reverend Elms,
Coæval near with that, all ragged shew,
Long lash'd by the rude Winds: Some rift half down
Their branchless Trunks: Others so thin a Top,
That scarce Two Crows could lodge in the same Tree.
Strange Things, the Neighbours say, have happen'd here:
Wild Shrieks have issu'd from the hollow Tombs,
Dead men have come again, and walk'd about,
And the Great Bell has toll'd, unrung, untouch'd.
(Such Tales their Chear, at Wake or Gossiping,
When it draws near to Witching Time of Night.)

Oft, in the lone Church-yard at Night I've seen
By Glimpse of Moon-shine, chequering thro' the Trees,
The School-boy with his Satchel in his Hand
Whistling aloud to bear his Courage up,

And lightly tripping o'er the long flat Stones
(With Nettles skirted, and with Moss o'ergrown,)
That tell in homely Phrase who lie below;
Sudden! he starts, and hears, or thinks he hears
The sound of something purring at his Heels:
Full fast he flies, and dares not look behind him,
Till out of Breath he overtakes his Fellows;
Who gather round, and wonder at the Tale
Of horrid *Apparition*, tall and ghastly,
That walks at Dead of Night, or takes his Stand
O'er some new-open'd *Grave*; and, strange to tell!
Evanishes at Crowing of the Cock.

THE REVD. ROBERT BLAIR, *The Grave*, 1743

WINTER SCENE

THE night was winter in his roughest mood;
The morning sharp and clear. But now at noon
Upon the southern side of the slant hills,
And where the woods fence off the northern blast,
The season smiles, resigning all its rage,
And has the warmth of May. The vault is blue
Without a cloud, and white without a speck
The dazzling splendour of the scene below.
Again the harmony comes o'er the vale;
And through the trees I view th'embattled tow'r
Whence all the music. I again perceive
The soothing influence of the wafted strains,
And settle in soft musings as I tread
The walk, still verdant, under oaks and elms,
Whose outspread branches overarch the glade.
The roof, though moveable through all its length
As the wind sways it, has yet well suffic'd,
And, intercepting in their silent fall
The frequent flakes, has kept a path for me.
No noise is here, or none that hinders thought.
The redbreast warbles still, but is content
With slender notes, and more than half suppress'd:
Pleas'd with his solitude, and flitting light
From spray to spray, where'er he rests he shakes
From many a twig the pendant drops of ice,
That tinkle in the wither'd leaves below.
Stillness, accompanied with sounds so soft,
Charms more than silence. Meditation here
May think down hours to moments. Here the heart
May give an useful lesson to the head,
And learning wiser grow without his books.

WILLIAM COWPER, *The Task*, 1785

A CURATE

Fashion, blind authoress of great abuse,
That starves the curate down to forty pounds,
Carpenter's wages; and anon in terms
Of loud invective rails against the Church,
For owning sons of ignorance and vice.
Who is to blame? The needy Curate? No,
How can he purchase knowledge? He must live.
What can he learn then? Kennicott alone
Would cost him eight weeks pay. What wonder, then,
He drops his learning, and becomes a dunce?
He gossips all day long, from house to house,
Dines where he can, and cares not where he dines,
Forsakes divinity, and is at best
A walking colander, for news and wine;
A travelling post who seldom sleeps at home,
Returning to his lodgings once a week,
Duly apparent with the Sunday sun,
And with the Sunday sun again withdrawn.
Perhaps if in some lonely village plac'd,
Remote from balls, assemblies, cards, and routs,
He hires a farm, and with amazing zeal
Preaches one day in seven, and ploughs the rest.
Who blames him? Destitute of pence and books,
How can he study? To be misemploy'd
Becomes him better than to lounge abroad,
In yawning idleness, the source of vice,
Which like a burr to ev'ry idler's coat
Closely adheres, and on the sable clerk
Is doubly visible.

THE REVD. JAMES HURDIS, *The Relapse*, 1810

HOLY THURSDAY

'Twas on a Holy Thursday, their innocent faces clean,
The children walking two & two, in red & blue & green,
Grey headed beadles walk'd before, with wands as white as
    snow,
Till into the high dome of Paul's they like Thames' waters
    flow.

O what a multitude they seem'd, these flowers of London
    town!
Seated in companies, they sit with radiance all their own.
The hum of multitudes was there, but multitudes of lambs,
Thousands of little boys & girls raising their innocent hands.

Now like a mighty wind they raise to heaven the voice of song,
Or like harmonious thunderings the seats of heaven among.
Beneath them sit the aged men, wise guardians of the poor;
Then cherish pity, lest you drive an angel from your door.

WILLIAM BLAKE, *Songs of Innocence*, 1789

THE CHURCH

"WHAT is a Church?"—Let Truth and Reason speak,
They would reply, "The faithful, pure, and meek;
From Christian folds, the one selected race,
Of all professions, and in every place."

    "What is a Church?"—"A flock," our Vicar cries,
"Whom bishops govern and whom priests advise;
Wherein are various states and due degrees,
The Bench for honour, and the Stall for ease;
That ease be mine, which, after all his cares,
The pious, peaceful prebendary shares."

    "What is a Church?"—Our honest Sexton tells,
" 'Tis a tall building, with a tower and bells;
Where priest and clerk with joint exertion strive
To keep the ardour of their flock alive;
That, by his periods eloquent and grave;
This, by responses, and a well-set stave:
These for the living; but when life be fled,
I toll myself the requiem for the dead . . ."

    But ere you enter, yon bold Tower survey,
Tall and entire, and venerably grey,
For time has soften'd what was harsh when new,
And now the stains are all of sober hue;
The living stains which Nature's hand alone,
Profuse of life, pours forth upon the stone:
For ever growing; where the common eye
Can but the bare and rocky bed descry;
There Science loves to trace her tribes minute,
The juiceless foliage, and the tasteless fruit;
There she perceives them round the surface creep,
And while they meet their due distinction keep;
Mix'd but not blended; each its name retains,
And these are Nature's ever-during stains . . .

Seeds, to our eye invisible, will find
On the rude rock the bed that fits their kind;
There, in the rugged soil, they safely dwell,
Till showers and snows the subtle atoms swell,
And spread th'enduring foliage;—then we trace
The freckled flower upon the flinty base;
These all increase, till in unnoticed years
The stony tower as grey with age appears;
With coats of vegetation, thinly spread,
Coat above coat, the living on the dead:
These then dissolve to dust, and make a way
For bolder foliage, nursed by their decay:
The long-enduring Ferns in time will all
Die and depose their dust upon the wall;
Where the wing'd seed may rest, till many a flower
Show Flora's triumph o'er the falling tower.

But ours yet stands, and has its Bells renown'd
For size magnificent and solemn sound;
Each has its motto: some contrived to tell,
In monkish rhyme, the uses of a bell;
Such wond'rous good, as few conceive could spring
From ten loud coppers when their clappers swing.

Enter'd the Church—we to a tomb proceed,
Whose names and titles few attempt to read;
Old English letters, and those half pick'd out,
Leave us, unskilful readers, much in doubt;
Our sons shall see its more degraded state;
The tomb of grandeur hastens to its fate . . .

THE REVD. GEORGE CRABBE, *The Borough*, 1810

THE SQUIRE'S PEW

A SLANTING ray of evening light
   Shoots through the yellow pane;
It makes the faded crimson bright,
   And gilds the fringe again:
The window's gothic frame-work falls
In oblique shadow on the walls.

And since those trappings first were new,
   How many a cloudless day,
To rob the velvet of its hue,
   Has come and passed away!
How many a setting sun hath made
That curious lattice-work of shade!

Crumbled beneath the hillock green,
   The cunning hand must be,
That carv'd this fretted door, I ween,
   Acorn, and *fleur-de-lis*;
And now the worm hath done her part
In mimicking the chisel's art.

In days of yore (as now we call)
   When the first *James* was king,
The courtly knight from yonder hall
   Hither his train did bring;
All seated round in order due,
With broidered suit and buckled shoe.

On damask cushions, set in fringe,
   All reverently they knelt:

Prayer-books, with brazen hasp and hinge,
    In ancient English spelt
Each holding in a lily hand,
Responsive at the priest's command.

—Now, streaming down the vaulted aisle,
    The sunbeam, long and lone,
Illumes the characters awhile
    Of their inscription stone;
And there, in marble hard and cold,
The knight and all his train behold.

Outstretched together, are expressed
    He, and my lady fair,
With hands uplifted on the breast,
    In attitude of prayer;
Long visag'd, clad in armour, he,—
With ruffled arm and bodice, she.

Set forth, in order as they died,
    The numerous offspring bend;
Devoutly kneeling side by side,
    As though they did intend
For past omissions to atone,
By saying endless prayers in stone.

Those mellow days are past and dim,
    But generations new,
In regular descent from him,
    Have fill'd the stately pew;
And in the same succession go,
To occupy the vault below.

And now, the polish'd, modern squire,
    And his gay train appear,
Who duly to the hall retire,
    A season, every year,—
And fill the seats with belle and beau,
As 'twas so many years ago.

Perchance, all thoughtless as they tread
    The hollow sounding floor,
Of that dark house of kindred dead,
    Which shall, as heretofore,
In turn, receive to silent rest,
Another and another guest,—

The feather'd hearse and sable train,
    In all its wonted state,
Shall wind along the village lane,
    And stand before the gate;
—Brought many a distant county through,
To join the final rendezvous.

And when the race is swept away,
    All to their dusty beds,
Still shall the mellow evening ray
    Shine gaily o'er their heads;
While other faces, fresh and new,
Shall occupy the squire's pew.

JANE TAYLOR, *Essays in Rhyme*, 1816

Tax not the royal Saint with vain expense,
With ill-matched aims the Architect who planned—
Albeit labouring for a scanty band
Of white-robed Scholars only—this immense
And glorious Work of fine intelligence!
Give all thou canst; high Heaven rejects the lore
Of nicely-calculated less or more;
So deemed the man who fashioned for the sense
These lofty pillars, spread that branching roof
Self-poised, and scooped into ten thousand cells,
Where light and shade repose, where music dwells
Lingering—and wandering on as loth to die;
Like thoughts whose very sweetness yieldeth proof
That they were born for immortality.

What awful pérspective! while from our sight
With gradual stealth the lateral windows hide
Their Portraitures, their stone-work glimmers, dyed
In the soft chequerings of a sleepy light.
Martyr, or King, or sainted Eremite,
Whoe'er ye be, that thus, yourselves unseen,
Imbue your prison-bars with solemn sheen,
Shine on, until ye fade with coming Night!—
But, from the arms of silence—list! O list!
The music bursteth into second life;
The notes luxuriate, every stone is kissed
By sound, or ghost of sound, in mazy strife;
Heart-thrilling strains, that cast, before the eye
Of the devout, a veil of ecstasy!

WILLIAM WORDSWORTH, *Ecclesiastical Sketches*, 1822

A PARSONAGE IN OXFORDSHIRE

WHERE holy ground begins, unhallowed ends,
Is marked by no distinguishable line;
The turf unites, the pathways intertwine;
And, wheresoe'er the stealing footstep tends,
Garden, and that domain where kindred, friends,
And neighbours rest together, here confound
Their several features, mingled like the sound
Of many waters, or as evening blends
With shady night. Soft airs, from shrub and flower,
Waft fragrant greetings to each silent grave;
And while those lofty poplars gently wave
Their tops, between them comes and goes a sky
Bright as the glimpses of eternity,
To saints accorded in their mortal hour.

WILLIAM WORDSWORTH, *Ecclesiastical Sketches*, 1822

THE VICAR

SOME years ago, ere time and taste
   Had turned our parish topsy-turvy,
When Darnel Park was Darnel Waste,
   And roads as little known as scurvy,
The man who lost his way between
   St. Mary's Hill and Sandy Thicket
Was always shown across the green,
   And guided to the Parson's wicket.

Back flew the bolt of lissom lath;
   Fair Margaret, in her tidy kirtle,
Led the lorn traveller up the path,
   Through clean-clipt rows of box and myrtle;
And Don and Sancho, Tramp and Tray,
   Upon the parlour steps collected,
Wagged all their tails, and seemed to say—
   "Our master knows you—you're expected."

Uprose the Reverend Dr. Brown,
   Uprose the Doctor's 'winsome marrow';
The lady laid her knitting down,
   Her husband clasped his ponderous Barrow;
Whate'er the stranger's caste or creed,
   Pundit or Papist, saint or sinner,
He found a stable for his steed,
   And welcome for himself, and dinner.

If, when he reached his journey's end,
   And warmed himself in Court or College,
He had not gained an honest friend
   And twenty curious scraps of knowledge,—

If he departed as he came,
  With no new light on love or liquor,—
Good sooth, the traveller was to blame,
  And not the Vicarage, nor the Vicar.

His talk was like a stream which runs
  With rapid change from rocks to roses:
It slipped from politics to puns,
  It passed from Mahomet to Moses;
Beginning with the laws which keep
  The planets in their radiant courses,
And ending with some precept deep
  For dressing eels, or shoeing horses.

He was a shrewd and sound Divine,
  Of loud Dissent the mortal terror;
And when, by dint of page and line,
  He 'stablished Truth, or startled Error,
The Baptist found him far too deep;
  The Deist sighed with saving sorrow;
And the lean Levite went to sleep,
  And dreamed of tasting pork to-morrow.

His sermon never said or showed
  That Earth is foul, that Heaven is gracious,
Without refreshment on the road
  From Jerome, or from Athanasius:
And sure a righteous zeal inspired
  The hand and head that penned and planned them,
For all who understood admired,
  And some who did not understand them.

He wrote, too, in a quiet way,
  Small treatises, and smaller verses,
And sage remarks on chalk and clay,
  And hints to noble Lords—and nurses;
True histories of last year's ghost,
  Lines to a ringlet, or a turban,
And trifles for the *Morning Post*,
  And nothings for Sylvanus Urban.

He did not think all mischief fair,
  Although he had a knack of joking;
He did not make himself a bear,
  Although he had a taste for smoking;
And when religious sects ran mad,
  He held, in spite of all his learning,
That if a man's belief is bad,
  It will not be improved by burning.

And he was kind, and loved to sit
  In the low hut or garnished cottage,
And praise the farmer's homely wit,
  And share the widow's homelier pottage:
At his approach complaint grew mild;
  And when his hand unbarred the shutter,
The clammy lips of fever smiled
  The welcome which they could not utter . . .

WINTHROP MACKWORTH PRAED,
  in *The New Monthly Magazine*, 1829

THE VILLAGE FANE

THE village fane its noble tower uprears,
Safe from the tempests of a thousand years;—
Still in their ancient strength these walls arise,
And brave the rudest shocks of wintry skies!
And see, within—how beautiful!—time-proof,
O'er aisle and nave light springs the embowed roof!
The massive door is open;—let me trace
With reverential awe the solemn place;—
Ah, let me enter, once again, the pew
Where the child nodded as the sermon grew;
Scene of soft slumbers! I remember now
The chiding finger, and the frowning brow
Of stern reprovers, when the ardent June
Flung through the glowing aisles the drowsy noon;
Ah, admonitions vain! a power was there
Which conquer'd e'en the sage, the brave, the fair,—
A sweet oppressive power—a languor deep,
Resistless shedding round delicious sleep!
Till, closed the learned harangue, with solemn look
Arose the chaunter of the sacred book,—
The parish clerk (death-silenced) far-famed then
And justly, for his long and loud—Amen!
Rich was his tone, and his exulting eye
Glanced to the ready choir, enthroned on high,
Nor glanced in vain; the simple-hearted throng
Lifted their voices, and dissolved in song;
Till in one tide rolling, full and free
Rung through the echoing pile, old England's psalmody.

NOEL THOMAS CARRINGTON, *My Native Village*, 1830

THE CELL BY THE SEA

How wildly sweet, by Hartland Tower,
　　The thrilling voice of prayer!
A seraph, from his cloudy bower
　　Might lean, to listen there.

For time, and place, and storied days,
　　To that great fane have given
Hues that might win an angel's gaze,
　　'Mid scenery of heaven.

Above—the ocean breezes sweep,
　　With footsteps firm and free:
Around—the mountains guard the deep,
　　Beneath—the wide, wide sea.

Enter! the arching roofs expand,
　　Like vessels on the shore;
Inverted, when the fisher band
　　Might tread their planks no more,

But reared on high in that stern form,
　　Lest faithless hearts forget
The men that braved the ancient storm,
　　And hauled the early net.

The tracery of a quaint old time
　　Still weaves the chancel screen:
And tombs, with many a broken rhyme,
　　Suit well this simple scene.

A Saxon font, with baptism bright,
    The womb of mystic birth,
An altar, where, in angels' sight,
    Their Lord descends to earth.

Here glides the spirit of the psalm,
    Here breathes the soul of prayer:
The awful church—so hushed—so calm—
    Ah! surely God is there.

THE REVD. ROBERT STEPHEN HAWKER, *Ecclesia*, 1840

ON SEEING OUR FAMILY-VAULT

THIS lodging is well chosen: for 'tis near
The fitful sighing of those chestnut trees;
And every Sabbath morning it can hear
The swelling of the hymnèd melodies;
And the low booming of the funeral bell
Shall murmur through the dark and vaulted room,
Waking its solemn echoes but to tell
That one more soul is gathered to its home.
There we shall lie beneath the trodden stone:—
Oh, none can tell how dreamless and how deep
Our peace will be, when the last earth is thrown,
The last notes of the music fallen asleep,
The mourners past away, the tolling done,
The last chink closed, and the long dark begun.

THE REVD. HENRY ALFORD, *Poetical Works*, 1845

BENEATH THE CHURCHYARD TREE

Yet, surely, when the level ray
    Of some mild eve's declining sun
Lights on the village pastor, grey
    In years ere ours had well begun—

As there—in simplest vestment clad,
    He speaks beneath the churchyard tree,
In solemn tones,—but yet not sad,—
    Of what Man is—what Man shall be!

And clustering round the grave, half hid
    By that same quiet churchyard yew,
The rustic mourners bend, to bid
    The dust they loved a last adieu—

That ray, methinks, that rests so sheen
Upon each briar-bound hillock green,
So calm, so tranquil, so serene,
Gives to the eye a fairer scene,—
Speaks to the heart with holier breath
Than all this pageantry of Death.

THE REVD. RICHARD HARRIS BARHAM,
The Ingoldsby Legends, 1840

THE DESERTED CHURCH

AFTER long travail on my pilgrimage,
I sat me down beside an aged heap,
For so it seem'd, with one square shatter'd keep,
Pensively frowning on the wrecks of age.
The river there, as at its latest stage,
Sinks in the verdure of its Sunday sleep,
And sings an under-song for them that weep
O'er the sad blots in life's too open page.
I look'd within, but all within was cold!
The walls were mapp'd with isles of dusky damp,
The long stalls look'd irreverently old,
The rush-strewn aisle was like a wither'd swamp,
And mark'd with loitering foot's unholy tramp;
The chancel floor lay thick with sluggish mould.

Hark! do you hear the dull unfrequent knell,
Survivor sad of many a merry peal,
Whose Sabbath music wont to make us feel
Our spirits mounting with its joyous swell,
That scaled the height, that sunk into the dell?
Now lonely, lowly swinging to and fro,
It warns a scatter'd flock e'en yet to go,
And take a sip of the deserted well.
And, dost thou hear?—then, hearing, long endure.
The Gospel sounds not now so loud and bold
As once it did. Some lie in sleep secure,
And many faint because their love is cold;
But never doubt that God may still be found,
Long as one bell sends forth a Gospel sound!

HARTLEY COLERIDGE, *Poems*, 1851

THE TWO CHURCHES

A HAPPY day, a happy year,
A zummer Zunday, dazzlèn clear,
I went athirt vrom Lea to Noke.
To goo to church wi' Fanny's vo'k:
The sky o' blue did only show
A cloud or two, so white as snow,
An' aïr did swäy, wi' softest strokes,
The eltrot roun' the dark-bough'd woaks.
O day o' rest when bells do toll!
A day a-blest to ev'ry soul!
How sweet the zwells o' Zunday bells.

An' on the cowslip-knap at Creech,
Below the grove o' steätely beech,
I heärd two tow'rs a-cheemèn clear,
Vrom woone I went, to woone drew near,
As they did call, by flow'ry ground,
The bright-shod veet vrom housen round,
A-drownèn wi' their holy call,
The goocoo an' the water-vall.
Die off, O bells o' my dear pleäce,
Ring out, O bells avore my feäce,
Vull sweet your zwells, O ding-dong bells.

Ah! then vor things that time did bring
My kinsvo'k, *Lea* had bells to ring;
An' then, ageän, vor what bevell
My wife's, why *Noke* church had a bell;
But soon wi' hopevul lives a-bound
In woone, we had woone tower's sound,

Vor our high jaÿs all vive bells rung,
Our losses had woone iron tongue.
Oh! ring all round, an' never mwoän
So deep an' slow woone bell alwone,
Vor sweet your swells o' vive clear bells.

THE REVD. WILLIAM BARNES, *Poems of Rural
Life in the Dorset Dialect,* 1862

LINCOLNSHIRE ADVICE

But Parson 'e *will* speäk out, saw, now 'e be sixty-seven
He'll niver swap Owlby an' Scratby fur owt but the Kingdom
o' Heaven;
An' thou'll be 'is Curate 'ere, but, if iver tha meäns to git
'igher,
Tha mun tackle the sins o' the Wo'ld an' not the faults o'
the Squire.
An' I reckons tha'll light of a livin' somewheers i' the Wowd
or the Fen,
If tha cottons down to thy betters, an' keeäps thysen to
thysen.
But niver not speäk plaain out, if tha wants to git forrards
a bit,
But creeäp along the hedge-bottoms, an' thou'll be a Bishop
yit.

ALFRED, LORD TENNYSON,
The Churchwarden and the Curate, 1892

OUR NEW CHURCH CLOCK

HENCEFORWARD shall our Time be plainly read—
Down in the nave I catch the twofold beat
Of those full-weighted moments overhead;
And hark! the hour goes clanging down the street
To the open plain! How sweet at eventide
Will that clear music be to toil-worn men!
Calling them home, each to his own fire-side;
How sweet the toll of all the hours till then!
The cattle, too, the self-same sound shall hear,
But they can never know the power it wields
O'er human hearts, that labour, hope, and fear;
Our village-clock means nought to steed or steer;
The call of Time will share each twinkling ear
With summer flies and voices from the fields!

THE PASTOR'S PRAYER

AT dawn, he marks the smoke among the trees,
From hearths, to which his daily footsteps go;
And hopes and fears and ponders on his knees,
If his poor sheep will heed his voice or no;
What wholesome turn will Ailsie's sorrow take?
Her latest sin will careless Annie rue?
Will Robin now, at last, his wiles forsake?
Meet his old dupes, yet hold his balance true?
He prays at noon, with all the warmth of heaven
About his heart, that each may be forgiven;
He prays at eve: and through the midnight air
Sends holy ventures to the throne above;
His very dreams are faithful to his prayer,
And follow, with clos'd eyes, the path of love.

THE REVD. CHARLES TENNYSON TURNER, *Sonnets*, 1873

AFTERNOON SERVICE AT MELLSTOCK

(Circa 1850)

ON afternoons of drowsy calm
    We stood in the panelled pew,
Singing one-voiced a Tate-and-Brady psalm
    To the tune of "Cambridge New."

We watched the elms, we watched the rooks,
    The clouds upon the breeze,
Between the whiles of glancing at our books,
    And swaying like the trees.

So mindless were those outpourings!—
    Though I am not aware
That I have gained by subtle thought on things
    Since we stood psalming there.

THOMAS HARDY, *Moments of Vision*, 1917

AFTER TRINITY

We have done with dogma and divinity,
    Easter and Whitsun past,
The long, long Sundays after Trinity
    Are with us at last;
The passionless Sundays after Trinity,
    Neither feast-day nor fast.

Christmas comes with plenty,
    Lent spreads out its pall,
But these are five and twenty,
    The longest Sundays of all;
The placid Sundays after Trinity,
    Wheat-harvest, fruit-harvest, Fall.

Spring with its burst is over,
    Summer has had its day,
The scented grasses and clover
    Are cut, and dried into hay;
The singing-birds are silent,
    And the swallows flown away.

Post pugnam pausa fiet;
    Lord, we have made our choice;
In the stillness of autumn quiet,
    We have heard the still, small voice.
We have sung *Oh where shall Wisdom?*
    Thick paper, folio, Boyce.

Let it not all be sadness,
    Not *omnia vanitas,*
Stir up a little gladness
    To lighten the *Tibi cras;*
Send us that little summer,
    That comes with Martinmas

When still the cloudlet dapples
    The windless cobalt blue,
And the scent of gathered apples
    Fills all the store-rooms through,
The gossamer silvers the bramble,
    The lawns are gemmed with dew.

An end of tombstone Latinity,
    Stir up sober mirth,
Twenty-fifth after Trinity,
    Kneel with the listening earth,
Behind the Advent trumpets
    They are singing Emmanuel's birth.

JOHN MEADE FALKNER
Poems, c. 1924

ANGLICAN ALPHABET

A is the Anglican brimfull of gas
B is the Breakfast he eats before Mass
C are the Curates at Cuddesdon bred
D are the Districts perambulated
E is the Eagle sublimely absurd
F are the Females who polish that bird
G is the Guild of the Church Lads' Brigade
H is the Helluva row that they made
I is the Incense we can't see our way to
J is St. Joseph they won't let us pray to
K is the Key to the Vicar's position
L is the Lace which we wear at the Mission
M is the Matins we have at eleven
N is the Nonsense we talk about Heaven
O is the Octave kept up with preaching
P is the Prayer Book, our standard of teaching
Q is the Quire of Communicant laymen
R is the Roar of the sevenfold Amen
S is the Stole all embroidered with lotuses
T is the Tone for giving out notices
U is the Use which we've had from our Aunt
V is the Vicar who says "No you can't"
W is the Wife whom our Vicar has wed
X the Uxorious life they have led.

Attributed to THE REVD. SANDYS WASON C. 1905

BELLS

What master singer, with what glory amazed,
Heard one day listening on the lonely air
The tune of bells ere yet a bell was raised
To throne it over field and flood? Who dare
Deny him demi-god, that so could win
The music uncreate, that so could wed
Music and hue—that, when the bells begin,
Song colours, colour sings? Beauty so bred
Enspheres each hamlet through the English shires
And utters from ten thousand peeping spires
(Or huge in starlight) to the outmost farms
Sweet, young, grand, old. The country's lustiest arms
Leap to the time till the whole sky retells
That unknown poet's masterpiece of bells.

EDMUND BLUNDEN, *English Poems*, 1925

CHURCH GOING

Once I am sure there's nothing going on
I step inside, letting the door thud shut.
Another church: matting, seats, and stone,
And little books; sprawlings of flowers, cut
For Sunday, brownish now; some brass and stuff
Up at the holy end; the small neat organ;
And a tense, musty, unignorable silence,
Brewed God knows how long. Hatless, I take off
My cycle-clips in awkward reverence,

Move forward, run my hand around the font.
From where I stand, the roof looks almost new—
Cleaned, or restored? Someone would know: I don't.
Mounting the lectern, I peruse a few
Hectoring large-scale verses, and pronounce
'Here endeth' much more loudly than I'd meant.
The echoes snigger briefly. Back at the door
I sign the book, donate an Irish sixpence,
Reflect the place was not worth stopping for.

Yet stop I did: in fact I often do,
And always end much at a loss like this,
Wondering what to look for; wondering, too,
When churches fall completely out of use
What we shall turn them into, if we shall keep
A few cathedrals chronically on show,
Their parchment, plate and pyx in locked cases,
And let the rest rent-free to rain and sheep.
Shall we avoid them as unlucky places?

Or, after dark, will dubious women come
To make their children touch a particular stone;
Pick simples for a cancer; or on some
Advised night see walking a dead one?
Power of some sort or other will go on
In games, in riddles, seemingly at random;
But superstition, like belief, must die,
And what remains when disbelief has gone?
Grass, weedy pavement, brambles, buttress, sky,

A shape less recognisable each week,
A purpose more obscure. I wonder who
Will be the last, the very last, to seek
This place for what it was; one of the crew
That tap and jot and know what rood-lofts were?
Some ruin-bibber, randy for antique,
Or Christmas-addict, counting on a whiff
Of gown-and-bands and organ-pipes and myrrh?
Or will he be my representative,

Bored, uninformed, knowing the ghostly silt
Dispersed, yet tending to this cross of ground
Through suburb scrub because it held unspilt
So long and equably what since is found
Only in separation—marriage, and birth,
And death, and thoughts of these—for whom was built
This special shell? For, though I've no idea
What this accoutred frowsty barn is worth,
It pleases me to stand in silence here;

A serious house on serious earth it is,
In whose blent air all our compulsions meet,
Are recognised, and robed as destinies.
And that much never can be obsolete,
Since someone will forever be surprising
A hunger in himself to be more serious,
And gravitating with it to this ground,
Which, he once heard, was proper to grow wise in,
If only that so many dead lie round.

PHILIP LARKIN, *The Less Deceived*, 1955

INDEX TO AUTHORS

Glasgow University Library